salsa

salsa

danceclub

paul bottomer

southwater

This edition is published by Southwater

Distributed in the UK by
The Manning Partnership
251–253 London Road East
Batheaston
Bath BA1 7RL
tel. 01225 852 727
fax 01225 852 852

Published in the USA by
Anness Publishing Inc.
27 West 20th Street
Suite 504
New York
NY 10011
fax 212 807 6813

Distributed in Canada by
General Publishing
895 Don Mills Road
400–402 Park Centre
Toronto, Ontario M3C 1W3
tel. 416 445 3333
fax 416 445 5991

Distributed in Australia by
Sandstone Publishing
Unit 1, 360 Norton Street
Leichhardt
New South Wales 2040
tel. 02 9560 7888
fax 02 9560 7488

Southwater is an imprint of Anness Publishing Limited
Hermes House, 88–89 Blackfriars Road, London SE1 8HA
tel. 020 7401 2077; fax 020 7633 9499

© Anness Publishing Limited 1996, 2002

Publisher: Joanna Lorenz
Senior Editor: Lindsay Porter
Photographer: Anthony Pickhaver
Make-up: Bettina Graham
Designer: Siân Keogh

Previously published as *Dance Crazy Salsa*

1 3 5 7 9 10 8 6 4 2

Contents

Introduction	6
The Musical Count	8
The Dance	9
What to Wear	10

Holds	11	Paseo	33
Basic Salsa Move	12	Armlock Turn to the Left	36
Getting the Salsa Feeling	14	Building up a Programme	40
Backwards Salsa Basic	16	Pachanga Heel Taps	41
Cucurachas	18	The Wrap	43
Forwards and Backwards Basic Move	20	Half Turns	46
Preparing to Turn	22	Half Turn and Changing Sides	49
Opening-out Movements	23	Extra Salsa Style	51
Figure of Eight	25	Pachanga Cross Swivels	54
Figure of Eight with Double Hand Hold	28	Armlock Turn to the Right	56
Changing Places Turn	31	Final Combination	60
Leading and Following	32	Further Information	64

Introduction

When in 1928 Ignacio Piñeiro used the phrase "Echale Salsita !" as the title of a new piece of music with lyrics, he could not have known the impact that that commonplace expression would have half a century later. Meaning "spice it up", the phrase was later simplified to "Salsa". Various singers and musicians included references to Salsa in their music and by the mid-1960s the Venezuelan radio presenter, Danilo Phidias Escalona, used the word in the title of his programme. It was not until the early 1970s that the phrase was recoined as a generic term for a diverse mixture of Latino music styles and rhythms previously known as "son"– guaracha danzón, cha cha cha, pachanga, rumba, mambo etc. This simple word suddenly made Latin music more marketable and demand for it took off. With the music, the dance inevitably followed.

The Latin countries of the Caribbean – Cuba, Puerto Rico, Haiti, the Dominican Republic and those of Central and South America – Mexico, Venezuela, and Colombia – share a common Latin culture and a fierce Latin pride. However, the influence and contribution of Afro-Caribbean music to Salsa is unmistakable. While many of the original styles of music were products of the Cuban countryside, economic necessity at various points in Cuba's history prompted migration to the cities, bringing the musical culture of the country into the towns. Like the Tango of Argentina, Salsa and its predecessors became a reflection of life in the *barrios* or poorer districts of town. Everyone could identify with it, and, in it, find an expression of their own, a reflection of their

life, or an opportunity to forget their mundane pre-occupations and lose themselves in the song, the rhythm and the dance.

Cuba's war of independence from 1868–78 against Spanish colonial rule virtually destroyed the important sugar industry and was followed in 1868 by the subsequent abolition of slavery. Afro-Cubans, having seen the destruction of their economic base, found their way into towns to seek ways to eke out a living. With them came the *Guajira*. At first the Guajira was considered vulgar, but it eventually gained acceptance and took its place in the unfolding story of Salsa.

Right: The popularity of today's vibrant Salsa scene shows no sign of waning.

Then came *Son,* a new style of Afro-Caribbean music which was to have a profound effect on the direction of all future Cuban music development. Son managed to combine the musical traditions of both Afro-Cuban and Latin-Cuban music in a new form which satisfied the people and which gained overwhelming popularity around the time of the First World War. The authorities, however, were not so happy about the lyrical themes which dwelt upon the privations of the ordinary people, and by 1917 Son was prohibited. But the popularity of the music and dance ensured their survival, and in 1920 the prohibition was revoked, with even the upper classes now captivated by its rhythm. Son continued to thrive through the next two decades, receiving even greater impetus after the Second World War with the advent of television. By this time though, other influences were beginning to bear on the original style of Son. During the 1930s, Jazz started to influence the purity of traditional Cuban music, and after the war, Jazz bands played Cuban music more in their own style than that of the Cubans. Perez Prado, originally, originally a Cuban, but then based in Mexico, managed to combine both the flavour of Cuba with the tradition of Jazz. The *danzón,* another Cuban dance, absorbed other rhythmic influences and its music, in the hands of Perez Prado, evolved into what we now call Mambo. In 1948, a new composition by Enrique Jorrín called *Engañadora,* suggested a new rhythm which was immediately siezed upon by the dancers and the Cha Cha Cha was born. When it was finally recorded and distributed in the early 1950s, its catchy rhythm assured its enduring popularity. In 1959, the revolutionary troops of Fidel Castro entered Havana. An era came to an end, and while many Cuban singers, musicians and composers chose to stay on, many also left; closing one chapter in Cuba and opening another in New York.

In New York, the music of Cuba became inextricably mixed with the musical variations of Puerto Rico and American Jazz. New styles of music were produced by new types of groups, bands and orchestras. Trombones found a place alongside trumpets, while traditional Caribbean instruments were retained in the rhythm sections, giving a wild new dimension to the development of Salsa. Then, in 1962, with the release of "Love Me Do", The Beatles changed everything. They became the new sensation of the era and as their fans grew, Latin music fell into decline. By the early 1970s, Fania records needed to promote their artists and repetoire. To do this they needed a name with which their product could be easily recognized, and so Salsa was born. Since those days however, the USA has not had the monopoly on Salsa nor on new innovations. Puerto Rico continues to be a major source of Salsa music, and the influence from Colombia has also been increasingly marked.

Left: In 1950s New York, trumpets were included in Salsa bands together with traditional Caribbean instruments.

The Musical Count

Salsa music generally has a rhythm of four equal beats in one musical bar. This is interpreted in the dance by three steps and a tap, corresponding to the four musical beats. However, as you progress from the more basic Salsa moves, the rhythm of four beats may be interpreted in the dance by only three steps per musical bar. In this case, the dancers will use a count of "quick, quick, slow". A "quick" equals one beat of music, while a "slow" equals two beats. This sounds complicated, especially to a beginner, but if you listen to the rhythm, you will quickly become accustomed to it and dancing in time will become second nature.

Occasionally you may see dancers dancing the first step of each movement on beat two, which means that the tap will have occurred on count one. This does not necessarily mean that they are dancing out of time with the music. Salsa is a distillation of a variety of music and dance styles. In some types of music, the second beat is accentuated and some dancers like to respond to this rhythmic accent. Because of the diversity of Salsa music, it is not possible to define a standard beat, one or two, on which the dance should start and, in any event, this is really more of a technical issue than one which would concern the beginner or the club dancer who is just out for a great time. It is much more important to get a feel for the music and then get out onto the floor and enjoy it.

The Moves

Because Salsa moves have often not been invented by professional dancers, they rarely have names. For the purposes of this book, descriptive titles for the figures have been invented or existing names for figures have been borrowed from other dances or styles. So do not be surprised if, in your own Salsa club, the dancers have no idea what you mean if you use names given in this book. On the other hand, if they do, it is probably because they have read the book, too.

The descriptions of the figures are not intended to indicate the only style used but are merely a basis for understanding the moves of a style seen in many of the Salsa clubs.

Left and above: Percussion instruments suchs as the bongos and maracas give Salsa music its rhythm.

The Dance

It is not clear how Salsa moves evolved or exactly where they came from. Salsa, as a dance, mirrors Salsa as a musical form. It is a distillation of many similar dances and rhythms. Inevitably, some moves were taken from traditional dances, some were adapted from other dance styles and some were invented. New moves are appearing all the time. The style of the dance is Afro-Caribbean, which gives a relaxed feel to the moves. The rhythm is a standard four beat repetition interpreted by the dancers changing weight on three counts, and either tapping on the fourth, or incorporating the fourth beat into the third to make a third slow count. The moves themselves are simple enough but, as is always the case in dancing, it's not what you do, it's the way that you do it. In Salsa, the upper body is held still and upright throughout the dance, while the hips swing and sway rhythmically as a result of the leg action used. Note that the hip movement is a by-product of a good leg action, rather than an action in itself.

▼1 The dancers step to the right or left on the first count. Their movements mirror one another.

▲2 The weight shifts onto the opposite foot...

▼3 ... and back to the first.

▲4 The last step is a tap.

What to Wear

What to wear can vary quite a lot. Friday and especially Saturday nights are the traditional times to dress up, so if you are visiting a Salsa club for the first time on a Saturday, then it's time to get out the glad rags. If, however, you are clubbing on a weekday evening, go dressed very casually. Men can wear jeans and a T-shirt, while women more often wear a short skirt rather than jeans or trousers. Men are often to be seen in trainers, but they are not to be recommended for dancing as they very quickly get hot, causing the feet to swell, and inhibit the leg action, making turns considerably more difficult. Light casual shoes are better. Remember that, even if your club is air-conditioned, it will get hot, so dress cool. An appropriately coloured handkerchief casually hanging from the back pocket of your jeans is not just a fashion item but a practical accessory. A towel will also come in very handy.

One good tip for women is to think about your hair. If you have long hair which is likely to fly out during a spin, tie it up or back to ensure that you avoid slapping your partner in the face. This will also keep you cooler.

Above: Men will probably find shoes other than trainers better for dancing.

hair is tied back, to make spinning easier

a sleeveless top will keep you cool

full skirts

shoes with heels, yet comfortable for dancing

Holds

There are two general types of hold in Salsa, one in which the couple are in close contact and the other in which the couple are dancing apart or in an open position.

▶ Close Contact Hold

The man holds the woman around the waist with the right hand. The right hand need not close against her back. The woman places her left hand on the man's upper right arm, shoulder, back or neck. Her right hand is in the man's left, at eye level. The woman stands slightly to the man's right, so his left foot is outside her right foot and his right foot is between her feet.

◀ Open Hold

This hold varies. The couple stand an arm's length apart. The woman's arms are toned, so when the man leads through the arm she feels it. They may hold hands, left to right, right to left, or take a double hold. In Cuban style, the man may hold the woman's wrist; in Colombian, double holds are preferred. If only one hand is used, the free arm should be flexed and held out to the side.

Basic Salsa Move

Take up a close contact hold. The man is standing with his weight on the right foot and the woman with her weight on the left foot. It is customary for the man to initiate the dance by dancing a left foot tap on count four. Keep the steps small and under the body; the objective is not to move around the floor in this move.

1 Man
Take a small step to the side onto the left foot.
Woman
Take a small step to the side onto the right foot.

2 Man
Move the right foot sideways towards the left foot (it is not necessary to close).
Woman
Move the left foot sideways towards the right foot (it is not necessary to close).

3 Man

Take a small step to the side onto the left foot.

Woman

Take a small step to the side onto the right foot.

▶4 Man

Tap the floor with the inside edge of the ball of the right foot.

Woman

Tap the floor with the inside edge of the ball of the left foot.

▶5 Man

Take a small step to the side onto the right foot.

Woman

Take a small step to the side onto the left foot.

6 Man

Move the left foot sideways towards the right foot (it is not necessary to close).

Woman

Move the right foot sideways towards the left foot (it is not necessary to close).

7 Man

Take a small step to the side onto the right foot.

Woman

Take a small step to the side onto the left foot.

▶8 Man

Tap the floor with the inside edge of the ball of the left foot.

Woman

Tap the floor with the inside edge of the ball of the right foot.

MUSIC SUGGESTION

"Yamulemao" by Joe Arroyo (World Circuit) is a popular Salsa with a steady and relaxed tempo – ideal for practising the Basic Salsa Moves.

Getting the Salsa Feeling

The Salsa feel is given to the basic movement by a combination of keeping the upper body perfectly still and concentrating the energy into the waist and legs. The leg action is all-important because it is this which gives the characteristic hip movement of the dance. However, this hip movement is a by-product of the correct leg action and is not an independent movement.

THE LEG ACTION

Let's look at the essential leg action using Steps 1–4 of the man's Basic Salsa Move. This is the same as Steps 5–8 for the woman. The same action is repeated on the remaining steps of the move, which go in the opposite direction.

1 Take a small step to the side onto the left foot. Do not lift the foot far from the floor but lightly skim it. Flex the left knee, so that only the inside edge of the ball of the left foot is in contact with the floor. Keep the right knee fairly straight but not rigid. Imagine that, as you lower your weight onto the left foot, you are encountering some resistance and are having to push the foot down onto the floor. As you transfer your weight onto the left foot, the left knee becomes straighter, while the right knee flexes slightly

2 Move the right foot sideways towards the left foot. The right knee is already flexed. Keep it flexed and move the right foot closer to the left without closing. Let the inside edge of the ball of the right foot rest on the floor. Imagine some resistance as you push down onto the right foot. As you transfer your weight onto the right foot, the right knee becomes straighter, and the left flexes.

3 Repeat Step 1.

4 Tap the floor with the inside edge of the ball of the right foot. The right knee is already flexed.

Elimating the Tap

In a number of moves, particularly when the body weight is moving forward or backwards, it is desirable to eliminate the tap. When this occurs, the third step of the musical bar becomes a "slow" count. However, to maintain the Salsa action, the foot is placed in position on the third count but the transfer of body weight onto the foot is delayed until the fourth count. This illustrates the importance of the tap occurring on count 4 rather than on count 1 as sometimes proposed. Count 4 is added to count 3 to become a "slow". If the tap were to occur on count 1 and count 1 were to join count 4 to become the "slow", then it would go over the bar of music and the dancer would be "out of rhythm".

Style Tip

Generally, the rule is that when the body weight is moved onto the foot in a Basic Action, the same knee will straighten a little amd the other knee will flex. When transferring body weight onto a foot, the body weight is never allowed to "drop" into place. The lowering is controlled through the knee and ankle to produce a feeling of "pumping" the legs. A good Basic Action is vital to Salsa, but it can be a little tricky to begin with. Practice not only makes perfect, it makes it possible, so practise until it becomes second nature. You can do this on your own without a partner but, with or without a partner, be sure to keep the upper body still. When practising alone, use your arms with your hands at waist height.

Backwards Salsa Basic

This is a useful move, used to initiate many other figures. The man has just tapped the left foot and the woman her right at the end of the last move. The man stands on the right foot and the woman on the left. To start this move, the man gently pushes the woman away into an open position.

1 Man

Move the left foot back, leaving the right foot in place, releasing the heel of the right foot and flexing the right knee. The left leg straightens as the body weight moves over the foot.

Woman

Move the right foot back, leaving the left foot in place, releasing the heel of the left foot and flexing the left knee. The right leg straightens as the body weight moves over the foot.

2 Man

Transfer your body weight forward onto the right foot, pressing the body weight onto the right foot. The right leg straightens as the body weight moves over the foot.

Woman

Transfer your body weight forward onto the left foot, pressing the body weight onto the left foot. The left leg straightens as the body weight moves over the foot.

▲ 3 Man

Close the left foot to the right foot using the Salsa action.

Woman

Close the right foot to the left foot using the Salsa action.

4 Man

Tap the inside edge of the ball of the right foot next to the left foot.

Woman

Tap the inside edge of the ball of the left foot next to the right foot.

5 Man

Move the right foot back, leaving the left foot in place, releasing the heel of the left foot and flexing the left knee. Straighten your right knee as you transfer your weight.

Woman

Move the left foot back, leaving the right foot in place, releasing the heel of the right foot and flexing the right knee. Straighten your left knee as you transfer your weight.

6 Man

Transfer your body weight forward onto the left foot, pressing the body weight onto the left foot. Straighten the left leg as you transfer your weight onto it.

Woman

Transfer your body weight forward onto the right foot, pressing the body weight onto the right foot. Straighten the right leg as you transfer your weight onto it.

7 Man

Close the right foot to the left foot using the Salsa action.

Woman

Close the left foot to the right foot using the Salsa action.

8 Man

Tap the inside edge of the ball of the left foot next to the right foot.

Woman

Tap the inside edge of the ball of the right foot next to the left foot.

Cucurachas

"Cucuracha" is the Latin-American Spanish word for "cockroach" and this move may derive its name from the action of stepping on such an insect. To dance the move, assume a double hand hold, as for the Backwards Salsa Basic. The man has just tapped the left foot and the woman the right foot at the end of the preceding move. The man is standing on the right foot and the woman on the left. To initiate this movement, the man firmly but gently pushes the woman away from him into an open position.

1 Man
Move to the side onto the left foot, leaving the right foot in place.
Woman
Move to the side onto the right foot, leaving the left foot in place.

2 Man
Replace your body weight onto the right foot, leaving the left foot in place.
Woman
Replace your body weight onto the left foot, leaving the right foot in place.

3 Man
Close the left foot to the right foot.
Woman
Close the right foot to the left foot.

▶ 4 **Man**
Tap the inside edge of the ball of the right foot next to the left foot.
Woman
Tap the inside edge of the ball of the left foot next to the right foot.

5 **Man**
Move to the side onto the right foot, leaving the left foot in place.
Woman
Move to the side onto the left foot, leaving the right foot in place.

6 **Man**
Replace your body weight onto the left foot, leaving the right foot in place.
Woman
Replace your body weight onto the right foot, leaving the left foot in place.

7 **Man**
Close the right foot to the left foot.
Woman
Close the left foot to the right foot.

8 **Man**
Tap the inside edge of the ball of the left foot next to the right foot.
Woman
Tap the inside edge of the ball of the right foot next to the left foot.

Forwards and Backwards Basic Move

This move can be danced in either a close contact hold or an open hold. If you are using a double hand hold, the man can resume the close contact hold by releasing the right hand and drawing the woman towards him as he draws closer to her during the last movement of the preceding figure. The man is standing on his right foot, and the woman on her left.

▼2 Man
Transfer your weight back onto the right foot, leaving the left foot in place.
Woman
Transfer your weight forward onto the left foot, leaving the right foot in place.

▲1 Man
Move onto the left foot, leaving the right foot in place.
Woman
Move back onto the right foot, leaving the left foot in place.

▲3 Man
Move the left foot back to the right foot (it is not necessary to close).
Woman
Move the right foot forward to the left foot (it is not necessary to close).

4 Man

Tap the inside edge of the ball of the right foot next to the left foot.

Woman

Tap the inside edge of the ball of the left foot next to the right foot.

▶ 6 Man

Transfer your body weight forward onto the left foot, leaving the right foot in place.

Woman

Transfer your body weight back onto the right foot, leaving the left foot in place.

7 Man

Move the right foot forward next to the left foot (it is not necessary to close).

Woman

Move the left foot back next to the right foot (it is not necessary to close).

8 Man

Tap the inside of the ball of the left foot next to the right foot.

Woman

Tap the inside of the ball of the right foot next to the left foot.

5 Man

Move back onto the right foot, leaving the left foot in place.

Woman

Move forward onto the left foot, leaving the right foot in place.

Style Tip

During the Forwards and Backwards Basic Move, the Salsa action should be used. However, the feel is slightly different when moving forward or backward. When you move forward, try rolling your body weight around the edge of your foot, starting with the inside edge of the ball of the foot and ending with the leg pressing against the outside edge of the foot. As your body weight moves onto the outside edge of the foot, straighten the knee a little. This has a feeling of "looping the hip" around the foot. Try the same action when moving backwards. Remember to use the ball of the foot and then the flat foot when your weight moves onto it.

Preparing to Turn

Having practised and become familiar with the various basic moves, it is now time to explore some of the basic variations as we get into some more serious Salsa.

Turns are a key component of Salsa and the best *Salseros* will generate a turning momentum during a preceding move so that it leads quite naturally into the turn. In a basic variation, this may be built up gradually by repeating a preceding move three or four times with the music, each time increasing the turning momentum and thus giving the woman a clear signal of what is to follow. The idea of repeating the same move occurs again and again in Salsa and reflects the often repetitive nature of the music in each musical phrase. By listening to the music, you will become accustomed to matching your dancing to the musical phrasing.

In this move, allow the natural movement of the figure to do the work for you, gradually building up into the next move and making the transition virtually effortless. Dance three of four Backwards Salsa Basics with the following modifications.

Below: On Step 5, the man should use the right hand to ease the woman gently backwards and away from him.

Above: On the next Step 1, the man places his right hand on the woman's left hip.

Below: On each successive Step 5, the man should gently but firmly push the woman's left side away and increase his own turn to the right.

Woman's Movements

On Step 5, allow the man to push you away from him, matching his turn. When the amount of turn has been developed to a point where the couple are moving backwards to a side-by-side position, you can move easily into the next figure.

Opening-out Movements

In this figure, we simply pick up on the momentum of the turns made during the Backwards Salsa Basic described opposite and develop it into an opening-out movement. The man is standing on the right foot and the woman on the left. The man now initiates a turn to mirror the opening out of the couple at the end of the Backwards Salsa Basic.

▼1 Man
Move back onto the left foot, making a quarter turn to the left. Move the right hand across the woman's lower back to accommodate the turn, which ends with the woman on your right side. (Count – quick)

Woman
Move back onto the right foot, making a quarter turn to the right. It is comfortable for the left arm to move across the man's upper back. End with the man on your left. (Count – quick)

▲2 Man
Transfer your body weight forward onto the right foot, starting to turn to the right. (Count – quick)

Woman
Transfer your body weight forward onto the left foot, starting to turn to the left. Allow the left hand to slide across the man's back. (Count – quick)

▼ 3 Man

Making a quarter turn to the right and leading the woman with your right forearm to face you, move to the side onto the left foot. Take up a hand-to-hand hold with the left hand or place the left hand around the woman's waist. (Count – slow)

Woman

Making a quarter turn to the left to face the man, move to the side onto the right foot. Move the right hand to the man's left arm. (Count – slow)

▲ 4 Man

Releasing the right hand, move back onto the right foot, making a quarter turn to the right. End with the woman on your left, standing side by side. (Count – quick)

Woman

Releasing the left hand, move back onto the left foot, making a quarter turn to the left. End with the man on your right, standing side by side. (Count – quick)

5 Man

Transfer your body weight forward onto the left foot, starting to turn to the left. (Count – quick)

Woman

Transfer your body weight forward onto the right foot, starting to turn to the right. (Count – quick)

6 Man ▲

Making a quarter turn to the left and leading the woman to face you, move to the side onto the right foot. Place the right hand around the woman's waist. (Count – slow)

Woman

Making a quarter turn to the right to face the man, move to the side onto the left foot. Move the left hand to the man's upper left arm. (Count – slow)

Style Tip

It is important on Step 6 for both the man and the woman to be facing each other squarely. The woman should not anticipate a repetition of the turn. It may be repeated or the man may choose to lead from this neutral position into a Backwards Salsa Basic, in which case he will take the woman's right hand in his left hand on Step 6.

Figure of Eight

In this figure, one dancer turns, while the other dances a basic move. In this way, the man and woman alternate their turns. Start by dancing Steps 1–4 of the Backwards Salsa Basic with a double hand hold. As the man and woman move backwards and away from each other on Step 1, the man changes the hold of his left hand by moving the palm to face upwards and lowering the hands to waist height. This is a clear signal, alerting the woman to the turn which will follow. The man's right hand releases the woman's left hand. At the end of Step 4, the man is standing on the left foot and the woman on the right foot, ready to change places in the Figure of Eight.

1 Man

Move back onto the right foot, leaving the left foot in place. Use the right hand to move the woman backwards and away from you, ensuring that the right hand is free. (Count – quick)

Woman

Move back onto the left foot, leaving the right foot in place, ensuring that the left hand is free. (Count – quick)

2 Man

Transfer your body weight forward onto the left foot, starting to turn to the left. Start moving the free right hand across your body above the joined hands. (Count – quick)

Woman

Transfer your body weight forward onto the right foot, starting to turn to the right. (Count – quick)

3 Man

Move to the side with the right foot, making a quarter turn to the left, ending with your back to the woman. Keep hold with the left hand.
(Count – slow)

Woman

Move to the side with the left foot, making a quarter turn to the right, ending facing the man's back. Keep hold with the right hand.
(Count – slow)

4 Man

Continue turning, making a further quarter turn to the left. Release hold with the left hand, and move back onto the left foot. Take the woman's left hand in your right hand.
(Count – quick)

Woman

Continue turning, making a further quarter turn to the right and move back onto the right foot, leaving the left foot in place. Hold the left hand at waist height.

5 Man

Transfer your body weight forward onto the right foot, starting to turn to the right, while leading the woman to turn anticlockwise in the same way as you turned on Step 2. (Count – quick)

Woman

Transfer your body weight forward onto the left foot, starting to turn to the left. Start moving the free right hand across your body above the joined hands.
(Count – quick)

6 Man

Move to the side with the left foot, making a quarter turn to the right, ending facing the woman's back. Keep hold with the right hand.
(Count – slow)

Woman

Move to the side with the right foot, making a quarter turn to the left, ending with your back to the man. Keep hold with the left hand.
(Count – slow)

▶7 Man

Continue turning clockwise, making a further quarter turn to the right. Release the right hand and move back onto the right foot, leaving the left foot in place. Take the woman's right hand in your left hand.
(Count – quick)

Woman

Continue turning anticlockwise, making a further quarter turn to the left. Release the left hand and move back onto the left foot, leaving the right foot in place. Hold the right at waist height.
(Count – quick)

MUSIC SUGGESTION

"Lloraras" and "Me Dejo" by Oscar D'Leon (Codiscos). Oscar D'Leon is one of the most popular artists on the international Salsa scene. "Lloraras" is a club favourite. "Me Dejo" is a little slower and excellent for practice.

8 Man

Transfer your body weight forward onto the left foot. At this point, take up an appropriate hold, depending on the next figure. (Count – quick)

Woman

Transfer your body weight forward onto the right foot. (Count – quick)

▶9 Man

Move the right foot forward next to the left foot. (Count – slow)

Woman

Move the left foot forward next to the right foot. (Count – slow) (Note how the tap has been eliminated by the "slow" count.)

Figure of Eight with Double Hand Hold

Once you have mastered the Figure of Eight, let's introduce a new hold. Start as for the basic version of the figure. The man is standing on the left foot and the woman on the right foot, having danced Steps 1–4 of the Backwards Salsa Basic. The double hand hold is retained but the man has the palms facing up and the woman has the palms facing down. Contact is maintained through the fingers and thumbs.

1 Man
Move back onto the right foot, leaving the left foot in place and gently but firmly using both hands to move the woman backwards and away from you.
(Count – quick)
Woman
Dance Steps 1–9 of the basic version of the Figure of Eight and accept the lead produced by the new arm movements.

2 Man
Transfer your body weight forward onto the left foot, starting to turn to the left Raise the right arm.
(Count – quick)

3 Man

Move to the side with the right foot, making a quarter turn to the left, ending with your back to the woman. Release hold with the left hand and bring the right hand down over your head to waist height. Keep holding the woman's left hand in your right hand. (Count – slow)

4 Man

Continue turning, making a further quarter turn to the left and move back onto the left foot, leaving the right foot in place. Take the woman's right hand in your left hand to resume a double hand hold. (Count – quick)

5 Man

Transfer your weight forward onto the right foot, starting to turn to the right, while leading the woman to turn anticlockwise by raising the left arm across the woman and above her head. (Count – quick)

6 Man

Move to the side with the left foot, making a quarter turn to the right, ending facing the woman's back. Release hold with the right hand and bring the left arm down to waist height on the woman's left side. (Count – slow)

7 Man

Continue turning clockwise, making a further quarter turn to the right. Resume a double hand hold and move back onto the right foot, leaving the left foot in place.
(Count – quick)

8 Man

Transfer your body weight forward onto the left foot. At this point, take up an appropriate hold, depending on the next figure.
(Count – quick)

9 Man

Move the right foot forward next to the left foot.
(Count – slow)

Combination

Once you have mastered the two versions of the Figure of Eight, you can put them together in a great combination. First dance Steps 1–7 of the Figure of Eight, followed by Steps 2–9 of the Figure of Eight with Double Hand Hold. On the dance floor this can look very slick and, as you work together with your partner, the dynamics of this combination will really make you feel that you are dancing and enjoying Salsa.

Changing Places Turn

Use a variation of part of the Figure of Eight to produce an important standard Salsa move that is often used as an exit to a preceding figure. After step 3, continue with step 5 of the Backwards Salsa Basic.

▼ 1 Man

Move back onto the left foot, leaving the right foot in place and holding the woman's right hand with your left hand, palm up. (Count – quick)

Woman

Move back onto the right foot, leaving the left foot in place. (Count – quick)

▲ 2 Man

Transfer your weight forward onto the right foot, starting to turn to the right, while leading the woman to turn anticlockwise by raising the left arm across the woman and above her head. (Count – quick)

Woman

Transfer your weight forward onto the left foot, starting to turn anticlockwise. (Count – quick)

▼ 3 Man

Move to the side with the left foot, making a quarter turn to the right, ending facing the woman's back. Bring the left arm down to waist height, turning the woman to face you. (Count – slow)

Woman

Turning to the left under the man's arm, step onto the right foot, ending facing the man. (Count – slow)

Leading and Following

In contrast to other dance styles, where a couple may be used to dancing together on a regular basis, Salsa is more frequently danced with a variety of partners. It is therefore very important for the man to be able to lead his partner clearly and comfortably.

Below: Leads should never be used to force the woman to dance a move. In achieving this, it is vital for the man to be clear and decisive to avoid confusion. The lead must be given at the appropriate time, neither too late nor too early. Leads should fit into the flow of the figure to maintain fluidity and clarity.

Left: If the man wants to turn the woman to her right, then the lead will be given when the man is moving back on his right foot.

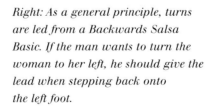

Right: As a general principle, turns are led from a Backwards Salsa Basic. If the man wants to turn the woman to her left, he should give the lead when stepping back onto the left foot.

Paseo

In this cheeky figure, the man and woman alternate spot turns. Dance a series of Forward and Backwards Basic Salsa movements. The tap on Step 4 is eliminated by dancing Step 3 to a "slow" count. When he is ready, the man leads the woman away from him on her backwards step and initiates the move by dancing a spot turn. Start in an open position without hold after the man has completed his Backwards Salsa Basic. He is now standing on the right foot facing his partner.

1–3 Woman
Dance a Backwards Salsa Basic. (Counts – quick, quick, slow)

1 Man
Move forward onto the left foot, leaving the right foot in place. (Count – quick)

2 Man
Make a half turn to the right on the left foot and transfer your body weight forward onto the right foot, ending with your back to the woman. (Count – quick)

3 Man

Move forward onto
the left foot, still
with your back to
the woman.
(Count – slow)

4 Man

Standing on the left
foot, swivel a half
turn to the right and
move back onto the
right foot, leaving
the left foot in place.
End facing the
woman.
(Count – quick)

Woman

Move forward onto
the left foot, leaving
the right foot in
place.
(Count – quick)

5 Man

Transfer your
weight forward onto
the left foot.
(Count – quick)

Woman

Make a half turn to
the right on the left
foot and transfer
your weight forward
onto the right foot,
ending with your
back to the man.
(Count – quick)

6 Man

Move forward onto
the right foot.
(Count – slow)

Woman

Move forward onto
the left foot, still
with your back to
the man.
(Count – slow)

7–9 Man

Dance a Forward Salsa Basic. (Counts – quick, quick, slow)

7 Woman

Standing on the left foot, swivel a half turn to the right and step backwards onto the right foot, leaving the left foot in place. End facing the man.
(Count – quick)

8 Woman

Transfer your body weight forward onto the left foot and resume the hold.
(Count – quick)

9 Woman

Move the right foot forward next to the left foot.
(Count – slow)

Armlock Turn to the Left

Another of the characteristic turns of Salsa, this typical move can be called the Armlock Turn for reasons which will become apparent as you dance through the steps. Start in a double hand hold. The man is standing on the right foot and the woman on the left foot.

▲ 1 Man

Move back onto the left foot, leaving the right foot in place. Lead the woman backwards and away from you, ready for the turn. (Count – quick)

Woman

Move back onto the right foot, leaving the left foot in place. (Count – quick)

▼ 2 Man

Transfer your body weight forward onto the right foot, turning slightly to the right. Gently depress the woman's right hand away from you, while raising the right arm and turning the woman's left hand away to initiate the woman's turn to the left. (Count – quick)

Woman

Transfer your weight forward onto the left foot, starting to turn to the left. (Count – quick)

▼3 Man

Move to the side onto the left foot, making a quarter turn to the right. Keep the right hand up and continue turning the woman in an anticlockwise direction. As the woman rolls into her right arm, the right arm will assume a position similar to an armlock. End holding the woman's left hand in your right hand with your right forearm across the woman's back. (Count – slow)

Woman

Move to the side onto the right foot, making a quarter turn to the left, ending with your back to the man. (Count – slow)

▲4 Man

Move back a small step onto the right foot, leaving the left foot in place. (Count – quick)

Woman

Make a further quarter turn to the left, allowing your right arm to move into the "armlock" position. Move back a small step onto the left foot, leaving the right foot in place. (Count – quick)

Style Tip

In step 3, the man should give the woman plenty of space for the rest of the figure.

▶ 5 Man

Transfer your body weight forward onto the left foot.
(Count – quick)

Woman

Transfer your body weight forward onto the right foot, starting to turn to the right.
(Count – quick)

6 Man

Move to the side onto the right foot, making a quarter turn to the left. Move the left hand to the left, leading the woman to unwrap. Lower the right hand to waist height.
(Count – slow)

Woman

Move back onto the left foot, making a half turn to the right.

▲ 7 Man

Move back onto the left foot, leaving the right foot in place. (Count – quick)

Woman

Move back onto the right foot, leaving the left foot in place. (Count – quick)

MUSIC SUGGESTION

"Que Bueno Baila Usted" by Oscar D'Leon (Rodven). This is a very catchy number with a feel and style particularly suitable for a Colombian interpretation. It is impossible to stand still to this track.

8 Man

Transfer your body
weight forward onto
the right foot.
(Count – quick)

Woman

Transfer your body
weight forward onto
the left foot.
(Count – quick)

9 Man

Move the left foot
forward next to the
right foot.
(Count – slow)

Woman

Move the right foot
forward next to the left
foot. (Count – slow)

*You can now
continue by
dancing into the
Backward Salsa
Basic. If you
wish to repeat
the Armlock
Turn, dance
Steps 1–7, then
Steps 2–9.*

Variation

On Step 4, it is possible for the man to
dance a Cucuracha onto the right foot.
Some men choose to dance back onto
the right foot with a quarter turn to the
right and then a quarter turn to the left
as they step back onto the left foot.
While the turn is possible, it can be
uncomfortable for the woman, as it
tightens the "armlock". The technique
described in the steps previously is
therefore preferable.

Building up a Programme

You can now try building up a short programme of the figures you have already learned. Of course, you can have fun making your own programme, but here's an example that you might like to try.

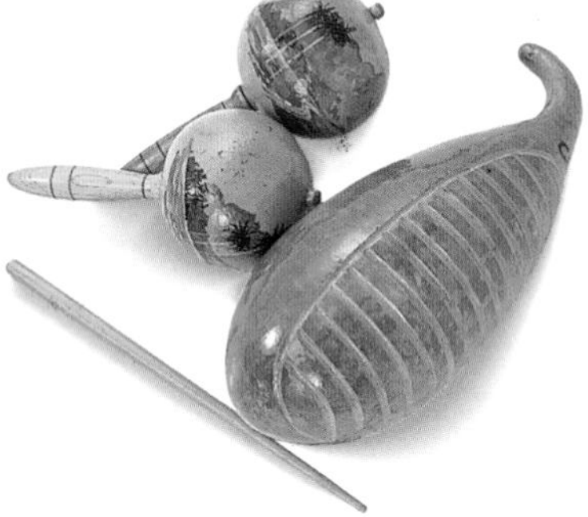

Basic Salsa Move (twice)

Cucurachas (twice)

Preparing to Turn

Opening-out Movements

Backwards Salsa Basic

Figure of Eight (Steps 1–7)

Figure of Eight with Double Hand Hold (Steps 2–7)

Figure of Eight with Double Hand Hold (Steps 2–9)

Armlock Turn to the Left (Steps 1–7)

Changing Places Turn

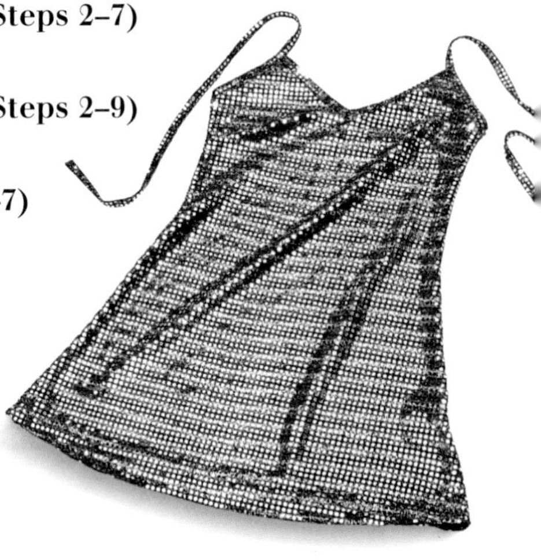

Pachanga Heel Taps

The Colombian style of Salsa places great emphasis on intricate footwork improvisations, which tend to make the Colombian style tighter than the Cuban style. Moves have always been borrowed from other dances, and here's one that has the exciting feel of the Pachanga.

Start in a double hand hold, palm to palm, and dance a complete Backwards Salsa Basic to a count of "quick, quick, slow, quick, quick, slow". On the last step, the man moves closer to the woman, but still without body contact, and he draws the woman towards him, moving his hand onto her waist and ensuring that she has transferred all of her weight onto the left foot. The toning of the woman's arms is critical in accepting the man's lead.

1 Man

Standing on the right foot, swivel a one-eighth turn to the right, then a three-eighths turn to the left with the knees together and the lower left leg held parallel to the floor. Lead the woman to turn by gentle pressure through the left hand and by turning her clockwise with the right hand. End touching the woman's raised foot with yours. (Count – & slow)

Woman

Standing on the left foot, swivel a one-eighth turn to the left, then a three-eighths turn to the right with the knees together and the lower right leg held parallel to the floor. If the man places his hand on your waist, respond by placing your left hand on his upper arm. End touching the man's raised foot with yours. (Count – & slow)

▶2 Man

Standing on the right foot, swivel a quarter turn to the right to face the woman and step onto the left foot. Lead the woman to face you by pulling her right hand to turn her right side forward and using your right hand to turn her at the waist.
(Count – slow)

Woman

Standing on the left foot, swivel a quarter turn to the left to face the man and step onto the right foot.
(Count – slow)

▶4 Man

Transfer your weight forward onto the left foot.
(Count – quick)

Woman

Transfer your weight forward onto the left foot.
(Count – quick)

▼3 Man

Step backwards onto the right foot, leaving the left foot in place to dance a Backwards Salsa Basic. Either release the right hand or resume a double hand hold. (Count – quick)

Woman

Step backwards onto the left foot, leaving the right foot in place to dance a Backwards Salsa Basic. (Count – quick)

5 Man

Move your right foot forward next to your left foot. (Count – slow)

Woman

Move your left foot forward next to your right foot. (Count – slow).

> *Continue with a Backwards Salsa Basic.*

The Wrap

When you have enjoyed a little practice at the turns and feel comfortable with them, try this new one. A right hand to right hand open hold is used throughout the Wrap. A useful way of adopting this hold while maintaining the flow of the movements is to dance a Changing Places Turn. On Step 3, the man transfers the woman's right hand into his own right hand. Dance Steps 5–8 of the Backwards Salsa Basic or Steps 5–7 to a "quick, quick, slow" rhythm. The man is now standing on the right foot and the woman on the left foot.

1 Man

Move back onto the left foot, leaving the right foot in place. Turning a little to the left will help the fluidity of the turn to follow and provide a signal to the woman. (Count – quick)

Woman

Move back onto the right foot, leaving the left foot in place. (Count – quick)

2 Man

Transfer your weight forward onto the right foot, starting to turn to the right. Draw the woman towards and across you and lead her to turn anticlockwise by depressing her right hand at waist height. (Count – quick)

Woman

Transfer your weight forward onto the left foot, starting to turn to the left. (Count – quick)

3 Man

Move forward onto
the left foot.
(Count – slow)

Woman

Move to the side
onto the right foot,
making a quarter
turn to the left to
end with your back
to the man. Your
right arm will have
been positioned by
the man ready for
the Wrap.
(Count – slow)

4 Man

Move a small step
forward onto the
right foot, leaving
the left foot in place.
Curve your right
hand, leading the
woman to continue
turning into your
right arm.
(Count – quick)

Woman

Move a small step
back onto the left
foot, leaving the
right foot in place
and turning a
quarter turn to the
left. Your right arm
will be wrapped.
(Count – quick)

5 Man

Transfer your
weight backward
onto the left foot.
Lower the joined
hands to enable the
woman to unwrap.
(Count – quick)

Woman

Transfer your body
weight forward onto
the right foot,
starting to turn to
the right.
(Count – quick)

6 Man

Move to the right
onto the right foot
and change hands to
take up a left hand
to right hand hold.
(Count – slow)

Woman

Step to the side onto
the left foot, making
a quarter turn
towards the man.
(Count – slow)

▶ 7 Man

Move back onto the left foot, leaving the right foot in place and turning to face the woman.
(Count – quick)

Woman

Move back onto the right foot, leaving the left foot in place and making a quarter turn to the right to end facing the man.
(Count – quick)

◀ 8 Man

Transfer your weight forward onto the right foot.
(Count – quick)

Woman

Transfer your weight forward onto the left foot.
(Count – quick)

▶ 9 Man

Move the left foot forward next to the right foot.
(Count – slow)

Woman

Move the right foot forward next to the left foot.
(Count – slow)

Neck Wrap

A great way of spicing up the Wrap is to dance it twice, including a Neck Wrap the second time. On Step 2, the man raises the right hand to neck height and leads the woman to turn into his right wrist. A good exit to this figure is to dance the Changing Places Turn using a right hand to right hand hold but with the man reverting to a left hand to right hand hold on Step 3.

Continue with Backwards Salsa Basic Movements or repeat Steps 1–6, then Steps 1–9.

Half Turns

The Half Turn is also known as the Cuddle Turn and you may decide to stay in the cuddle for a while before reluctantly exiting. Start in a double hand hold.

1 Man

Move back onto the left foot, leaving the right foot in place. Lead the woman backwards and away from you ready for the turn. (Count – quick)

Woman

Move back onto the right foot, leaving the left foot in place. (Count – quick)

2 Man

Move your body weight forward onto the right foot. Lead the woman to turn to her left by raising your left hand and drawing it towards the right across yourself and above the woman's head. Keep the right hand at waist height, leading the woman to turn into your right arm. (Count – quick)

Woman

Move your body weight forward onto the left foot, starting to turn to the left. (Count – quick)

3 Man

Move forward onto the left foot with the left arm still raised, turning to the right.
(Count – slow)

Woman

Move to the side onto the right foot, making a quarter turn to the left.
(Count – slow)

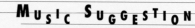

MUSIC SUGGESTION

"Mexico, Mexico" by Grupo Niche (Sony). This track, with its medium-fast tempo for the more experienced dancer, proved a hit for this popular group. For a fabulous blend of African and Caribbean rhythms, try "Africando" and "Yay Boy" by Africando (Stern's Africa). These tracks not only illustrate the common ancestry of Salsa, but are also great to dance to.

4 Man

Move forward onto the right foot, leaving the left foot in place. Lower the left hand to waist height in front of the woman to continue turning her. End in a side-by-side position with the woman on your right, your right hand holding the woman's left hand and your right forearm across her back. (Count – quick)

Woman

Move back, a small step, onto the left foot, leaving the right foot in place and making a further quarter turn to the left. End in a side-by-side position with the man on your left. (Count – quick)

5 Man

Move your body weight backwards onto the left foot and use your right forearm to lead the woman forward. Raise the left hand to allow the woman to pass beneath it.
(Count – quick)

Woman

Move your body weight forward onto the right foot, starting to turn to the right. (Count – quick)

▶ 6 Man

Move the right foot backwards next to the left foot. Lower the left hand to the normal position as the woman ends facing you.
(Count – slow)

Woman

Move to the side and back onto the left foot, making a quarter turn to the right.
(Count – slow)

▶ 8 Man

Transfer your body weight forward onto the right foot. (Count – quick)

Woman

Transfer your body weight forward onto the left foot. (Count – quick)

7 Man

Move the left foot back, leaving the right foot in place. (Count – quick)

Woman

Move back onto the right foot, leaving the left foot in place and making a quarter turn to the right. (Count – quick)

▲ 9 Man

Move the left foot forward next to the right foot. (Count – slow)

Woman

Move the right foot forward next to the left foot. (Count – slow)

> *Steps 7–9 may be replaced with the Changing Places Turn, which makes a good exit.*

Half Turn and Changing Sides

This figure, also known as the Double Cuddle, is great fun. Dance Steps 1–4 of the Half Turns before continuing into the new move.

1 Man
Return you body weight back to the left foot, keeping both hands at waist height. (Count – quick)

Woman
Move your body weight forward onto the right foot. (Count – quick)

2 Man
Move to the side onto the right foot, crossing behind the woman and leading her to move across in front of you to the left by slightly extending the arms and moving the woman within their frame. Position the woman slightly forward of a side-by-side position on your left. (Count – slow)

Woman
Move to the side onto the left foot, crossing in front of the man to end slightly forward of a side-by-side position with the man on your right. (Count – slow)

3 Man

Move forward onto the left foot, leaving the right foot in place. End standing in a side-by-side position with the woman on your left.
(Count – quick)

Woman

Move back onto the right foot, leaving the left foot in place. End standing in a side-by-side position with the man on your right.
(Count – quick)

4 Man

Transfer your weight back onto the right foot, leading the woman to transfer her weight forward.
(Count – quick)

Woman

Transfer your body weight forward onto the left foot.
(Count – quick)

5 Man

Move to the side onto the left foot, crossing behind the woman and leading her to move across in front of you to the right by slightly extending the arms and moving the woman within their frame. Position the woman slightly forward of a side-by-side position on your right.
(Count – slow)

Woman

Move to the side onto the right foot, crossing in front of the man to end slightly forward of a side-by-side position with the man on your left.
Count – slow)

6 Man

Move forward onto the right foot, leaving the left foot in place.

Woman

Move forward onto the left foot, leaving the right foot in place.

> *Continue with Step 5 of the Half Turns or stay in the Cuddle by repeating the move, remembering to include step 4 of the Half Turn.*

Extra Salsa Style

You can liven up some quite basic moves by incorporating some exotic extras. Try the first moves without overdoing them, then build them up to their full dramatic effect when you feel comfortable.

HALF TURN WITH BRAZILIAN HEAD THROW

Add a little extra "salsita" to the Half Turn by using an extra Brazilian Style point. This deliciously exotic move occurs on Step 4 of the Half Turn. When the woman moves back onto the left foot, she can perform a head throw by throwing her head back and lifting her right foot to knee height, pointing the toes to the floor. To facilitate this action, the man will replace his forward movement with a quarter turn to the right, extending the right leg straight, to create a "lunge line". A strong lead will be needed from the man's left hand while his right arm supports the woman. Try this first without overdoing it, then build up to the full extent for a special and fabulous effect.

SHIMMY

Try dancing a Forwards and Backwards Salsa Basic, with the man holding only the woman's right hand in his left hand. On the forward step, the dancers may choose to lean into the step to perform a Shimmy. In the Shimmy, alternate shoulders are moved rapidly forwards and backwards. When this occurs, the dancer who is moving back will incline their body backwards to match that of their partner.

Shimmies may also be incorporated into the Paseo for a special effect.

CHANGING PLACES TURN WITH OVERHEAD CUBAN SINK

You might want to spice the Changing Places Turn up a little. Here, the man starts the figure with a double hand hold, but brings his hands together so that they are touching. This hold is maintained while the woman turns under the hands. This is just the right moment for the Overhead Cuban Sink.

1 Man

Move to the side onto the right foot, leaving the left foot in place and maintaining the touching double hand hold.
(Count – quick)

Woman

Move to the side onto the left foot in a double hand hold with the hands held together.
(Count – quick)

2 Man

Move back onto the left foot with hands still together.
(Count – quick)

Woman

Move back onto the right foot with hands still together.
(Count – quick)

▽3 Man

Transfer your body weight forward onto the right foot with the arms now extended directly overhead and hands together, drawing the woman into a close contact hold. Sink well down into the right knee, while bringing the woman's hands down over your head and onto the back of your neck. (Count – slow)

Woman

Transfer your body weight forward onto the left foot. The arms will now be overhead and the man will resume a close contact hold. Sink well down into the left knee, allowing the man to bring your hands down over his head and onto the back of his neck. (Count – slow)

▽4 Man

Move to the side onto the left foot, lowering well into the right knee and rolling your body weight anticlockwise in a circular hip roll. (Count – quick)

Woman

Move to the side onto the right foot, lowering well into the left knee and rolling your body weight anticlockwise in a circular hip roll. (Count – quick)

▲ 5 Man

Continue the hip roll, allowing your body weight to move onto the right foot, while resuming a standard close contact hold. (Count – quick)

Woman

Continue the hip roll, allowing your body weight to move onto the left foot, while a standard close contact hold is resumed. (Count – quick)

▲6 Man

Close the left foot to the right foot. (Count – slow)

Woman

Close the right foot to the left foot. (Count – slow)

Pachanga Cross Swivels

Time now for some more captivating, complex Colombian moves, featuring a little tricky footwork for those so far undaunted. Again, we borrow a move from the exotic Pachanga. Dance a Backwards Salsa Basic in a double hand hold. The man is now standing on the right foot and the woman on the left foot.

1 Man
Standing on the right foot, swivel a little to the right, pointing the left toes towards the right toes and holding the left foot clear of the floor.
(Count – quick)
Woman
Standing on the left foot, swivel a little to the left, pointing the right toes towards the left toes and holding the right foot clear of the floor.
(Count – quick)

2 Man
Standing on the right foot, swivel a little to the left, bringing the left foot to cross the lower right leg and holding the left foot clear of the floor. (Count – quick)
Woman
Standing on the left foot, swivel a little to the right, bringing the right foot to cross the lower left leg and holding the right foot clear of the floor. (Count – quick)

3 Man

Pointing the left foot at your partner, move the left foot across the right foot and stand on the left foot.
(Count – slow)

Woman

Pointing the right foot at your partner, move the right foot across the left foot and stand on the right foot.
(Count – slow)

4 Man

Standing on the left foot, swivel a little to the left, pointing the right toes towards the left toes and holding the right foot clear of the floor.
(Count – quick)

Woman

Standing on the right foot, swivel a little to the right, pointing the left toes towards the right toes and holding the left foot clear of the floor. (Count – quick)

5 Man

Standing on the left foot, swivel to the right, bringing the right foot to cross the lower left leg and holding the right foot clear of the floor. (Count – quick)

Woman

Standing on the right foot, swivel to the left, bringing the left foot to cross the lower right leg and holding the left foot clear of the floor.
(Count – quick)

6 Man

Pointing the right foot at your partner, move the right foot across the left foot and stand on the right foot.
(Count – slow)

Woman

Pointing the left foot at your partner, move the left foot across the right foot and stand on the left foot. (Count – slow)

Armlock Turn to the Right

This figure is the same as the Armlock Turn learned earlier, but with the woman turning to the right rather than to the left. Start in a double hand hold, the man standing on the left foot and the woman on the right foot.

▲1 Man

Move back onto the right foot, leaving the left foot in place. Lead the woman backwards and away from you, ready for the turn. (Count – quick)

Woman

Move back onto the left foot, leaving the right foot in place. (Count – quick)

▼2 Man

Transfer your body weight forward onto the left foot, turning slightly to the left. Gently depress the woman's left hand away from you, while raising the left arm and turning the woman's left hand away to initiate the woman's turn to the right. (Count – quick)

Woman

Transfer your body weight forward onto the right foot, starting to turn to the right. (Count – quick)

▼ 4 Man

Move back a small step onto the left foot, leaving the right foot in place. (Count – quick)

Woman

Make a further quarter turn to the right, allowing your left arm to move into the "armlock" position. Take a step backwards onto the right foot, leaving the left foot in place. (Count – quick)

▲ 3 Man

Move to the side onto the right foot, making a quarter turn to the left. Keep the left hand up and continue turning the woman in a clockwise direction. As the woman rolls into her left arm, she will assume a position similar to an armlock. End holding the woman's right hand in your left hand. (Count – slow)

Woman

Move to the side onto the left foot, making a quarter turn to the right, ending with your back to the man. (Count – slow)

▲ 5 Man

Transfer your weight forward onto the right foot, starting to turn right. (Count – quick)

Woman

Transfer your body weight forward onto the left foot, starting to turn to the left. (Count – quick)

Dance Tip

Give the woman plenty of space for the rest of the figure.

6 Man

Move to the side onto the left foot, moving the right hand to the right and leading the woman to unwrap. Keep the left hand up. (Count – slow)

Woman

Move to the side onto the right foot, making a quarter turn to the left. (Count – slow)

7 Man

Move back onto the right foot, leaving the left foot in place and making a quarter turn to the right. (Count – quick)

Woman

Continue to make a further quarter turn to the left, moving back onto the left foot and leaving the right foot in place. (Count – quick)

8 Man

Transfer your body
weight forward onto
the left foot.
(Count – quick)

Woman

Transfer your body
weight forward onto
the right foot.
(Count – quick)

Combinations

As you build up your vocabulary of figures, you will want to experiment with
new combinations. To start with, try
interspersing the figures with basic
moves to give yourself thinking time. As
you become more competent, you will
find that you quite naturally move from
one figure to another without the need
for the basic moves. Remember,
though, that basic moves can be used to
build up momentum and aid the flow
into a following figure, which is especially helpful to an unfamiliar partner.

9 Man

Move the right foot
forward next to the
left foot.
(Count – slow)

Woman

Move the left foot
forward next to the
right foot.
(Count – slow)

Final Combination

We have seen how Salsa is a distillation of many dances and styles. In our final combination, we borrow a slow Merengue Turn from the Dominican Republic, the Alemana Turn from the Cuban rumba and include some sensuous Salsa Hip Rocks in a close Neck Wrap.

Start by dancing three steps of the standard Backwards Salsa Basic without taps. The man is standing on the right foot and the woman on the left foot.

BACKWARDS SALSA BASIC WITHOUT TAPS

1 Man
Move back onto the left foot, leaving the right foot in place.
(Count – quick)
Woman
Move back onto the right foot, leaving the left foot in place.
(Count – quick)

2 Man

Transfer your body
weight forward onto
the right foot.
(Count – quick)

Woman

Transfer your body
weight forward onto
the left foot.
(Count – quick)

3 Man

Close the left foot to
the right foot.
(Count – slow)

Woman

Close the right foot
to the left foot.
(Count – slow)

Merengue Turn

The man dances a Basic Salsa Move to
a count of "quick, quick, slow, quick,
quick, slow", eliminating the taps. He
steps to the right on the first three steps
and to the left on the last three steps,
ending standing on the left foot. He
leads the woman's turn by raising the
left arm and circling the left hand.

The woman starts with the left foot .
She dances six very small steps forward
in a circle, turning to the right with the
all-important Salsa action, pressing
down into the floor to produce a pumping action in the knees. She ends facing
the man and standing on the right foot.

ALEMANA TURN

▼ 1 Man

Move back onto the right foot,
leaving the left foot in place. Lead
the woman to turn to the right but
keep your left hand at neck height.
(Count – quick)

Woman

Making a quarter turn to the right,
step forward onto the left foot,
leaving the right foot in place.
(Count – quick)

▼ 3 Man

Move to the side onto the right foot,
allowing the woman to rotate into
your left hand in a Neck Wrap.
(Count – slow)

Woman

Step forward onto the left foot
between the man's feet in a Neck
Wrap hold. (Count – slow)

▲ 2 Man

Transfer your body weight forward
onto the left foot, still turning the
woman and keeping the left hand at
neck height. (Count – quick)

Woman

Standing on the left foot, make a half
turn to the right and transfer your
body weight forward onto the right
foot. (Count – quick)

HIP ROCKS

The Hip Rocks have a gyratory movement and are danced in the Neck Wrap hold. The knees are flexed and are positioned between your partner's knees.

▽ 1 Man

Flex the knees and step to the side onto the left foot with a circular movement of the hips. (Count – quick)

Woman

Flex the knees and step to the side onto the right foot with a circular movement of the hips. (Count – quick)

△ 2 Man

Transfer your body weight onto the right foot, continuing to make a circular movement with the hips. (Count – quick)

Woman

Transfer your body weight onto the left foot, continuing to make a circular movement with the hips. (Count – quick)

3 Man

Transfer your body weight onto the left foot. (Count – slow)

Woman

Transfer your body weight onto the right foot. (Count – slow)

The Exit

The man dances a Backwards Salsa Basic without the tap but, on the third step, he moves forwards on the right foot. As the movement starts, he encourages the woman to unwrap by a gentle but firm pull of the left hand.

The woman, turning to the left, takes forward walks on the left foot, then the right foot, before stepping back onto the left foot. The count is, of course, quick, quick, slow,

We hope that you have had some fun with this introduction to Salsa. You are sure to have much more fun in the future as you put the moves together into practice on the dance floor. Remember to relax, listen to the rhythm, enjoy the music and, or course, have fun dancing. Now, go for it and "echale salsita"!

Further Information

As your repertoire of moves increases and you feel
more comfortable and confident dancing them, why not
build on your experience by enrolling in a Salsa class? If you
feel you are ready, you could try out what you have
learned at your nearest Salsa club. If you are nervous, just
try to relax, enjoy the music and start with the basics.

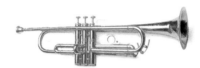

ACKNOWLEDGEMENTS

The author and publishers would like to thank the following for their participation in the
photography of this book:
Andrew Barrett, Tanya Janes, Luis Libres Bittencourt, Mina di Placido and Karina Rebelo

AUTHOR'S ACKNOWLEDGEMENTS

I would like to dedicate this book to Tanya Janes, my excellent partner, friend, companion and
guide to the Salsa club scene. Her modesty, tireless patience, good humour, enthusiasm and
encouragement in helping me to refine my understanding of the dance and research this book
were more valuable than words can convey and made the work terrific fun.
I owe Tanya both my thanks and my respect.

Thanks too to the people whose friendly welcome to Salsa clubs and whose enthusiasm for the
music and love of the dance were an object lesson in what dancing is really all about.

PUBLISHERS' NOTE

Dancing is great fun and an excellent form of exercise, but beginners should take care to start off
gently and work their way up to more advanced moves.